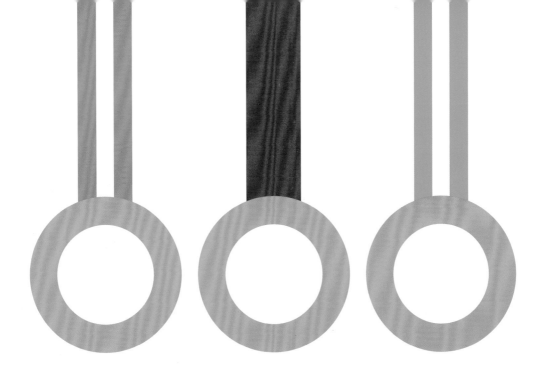

The London Games in Motion

Transport for London and the 2012 Olympics and Paralympics

D0294194

MAYOR OF LONDON

Transport for London

Contents

Introduction: Boris Johnson

London 2012 was a spectacular summer of success, and while Team GB and ParalympicsGB hauled in a trove of Gold, Silver and Bronze medals, many organisations throughout the Capital also turned in their own sparkling performances. Transport for London was at the heart of that success. Across the organisation hard work and meticulous preparation supported a magnificent Games, proved the gloomsters and doom-mongers wrong, and kept Londoners and London moving.

In fact, Transport for London notched up many 'personal bests', with the travel network never busier in all its 149-year history. Passenger numbers on the Tube rose 35 per cent above normal, while demand for London Overground services rose 47 per cent and Docklands Light Railway passenger numbers almost doubled. Tuesday 7 August proved the record breaker, with more than 4.5 million passengers taking the Tube.

The efficiency of our public transport network helped London to deliver a warm welcome to our visitors. More than 300,000 international and 600,000 UK sports and culture fans swelled our hotels to 84 per cent occupancy, double that achieved during the Beijing or Sydney Olympics. An incredible 5.5 million day visitors added to the festival atmosphere. Their positive experiences have heightened the Capital's reputation, and will benefit London's businesses and tourism and help drive jobs and growth for years to come.

Transport for London played a key role in making London 2012 remarkable for all the right reasons. To each member of staff I say thank you for your effort, your dedication and your hard work. We lived through an exciting, unforgettable summer in 2012, and much of that success belongs to you.

Boris Johnson, Mayor of London

Foreword: Sir Peter Hendy, CBE

Preparing any city's transport networks for the two biggest events on the planet, while running a service that allows for 'business as usual', is an undoubted challenge.

From the earliest days of the Olympic and Paralympic bid we knew a formidable task lay ahead. Yet the opportunities were enormous. We could advance our plans to develop east London's transport links, increase the accessibility of our services, regenerate overcrowded or rundown stations, and upgrade parts of the Overground and Tube.

Carrying out £6.5bn of works does not come without disruption. Some inconvenience to passengers and Londoners was, at times, unavoidable. We are grateful for their patience, which helped us complete our improvements within budget and to time.

The success of our Games transport plans also depended on our regular customers' cooperation. A third of Londoners and regular commuters heeded our *Get Ahead of the Games* messages and changed how and where they travelled.

We also received excellent support from London's businesses, and the freight and distribution industries: while we provided the information and online planning tools, it was businesses and their staff that adapted their routines, ensuring London kept moving and stayed stocked.

Getting London's transport network 'Games ready' depended on a collaborative partnership between us, the Mayor, the Olympic Delivery Authority, the London 2012 Organising Committee, London Boroughs, the Department for Transport, the Highways Agency, Network Rail, train-operating companies, the Traffic Commissioners, the Metropolitan Police and the British Transport Police, and our other transport partners.

That collective teamwork included setting up a single, dedicated Transport Coordination Centre, which ensured we provided high-quality, dependable travel advice to passengers throughout the Games.

People will remember the Games because of the outstanding sporting performances they witnessed. Yet equally memorable was the spirit of friendliness and helpfulness shown both by our volunteers and regular staff: our Travel Ambassadors; Incident Customer Service Assistants; station teams; and Tube, train and bus drivers. Together they represented not just the best of Transport for London, but the best of London as a world city.

To all our passengers and users, business partner organisations, and particularly to our staff and those of our contractors, thank you for making transport for the London 2012 Olympic and Paralympic Games such a resounding success.

Sir Peter Hendy, CBE
Commissioner, Transport for London

Accessibility

Most stations

on the Victoria line have level access platform to train

8,500 accessible buses

22,000 accessible taxis

16 stations had manual boarding ramps

66 step-free Tube stations

Travel Advice

3,200 Travel Ambassadors volunteered to help people travel in London

148,000 Twitter followers gained for TfL and GAOTG

60million travel-advice emails sent during the Games

 62,854,203 journeys planned using the Spectator Journey Planner during the Games

16% Total decrease in road traffic in central and inner London

70% of time the Games lanes remained open

77% of freight operators prepared for the Games

 25,000 businesses attended information sessions on how transport would be affected during the Games

250,000 business travel-advice packs distributed

2.6m spectators visited the Spectator Journey Planner

215,000 magenta wayfinding signs were installed

Athletes, Spectators and The Games

16,000
Olympics

7,500
Paralympics

Number of competing athletes and team officials

204
competing
nations
Olympics

167
competing
nations
Paralympics

26
Olympic
sports

20
Paralympic
sports

12
Number of
Olympic
venues in
London

97%
of athletes
expected to be
within 30 minutes
of their event

80%
of athletes
expected to be
within 20 minutes
of their event

---

15 Road events in
central London

1.8m
spectators
watched the
Olympic road
events

**Almost
10million**
Number of ticketed spectators
expected to attend the Games

100%
of spectators
expected to arrive
at the Games by
public transport

80%
of spectators
expected to
arrive at the
Games by rail

Winning the bid

- On 6 July 2005 at its 117th Session in Singapore, the International Olympic Committee awarded London the right to host the Games of the 30th Olympiad.
- London was the first city to host the Games three times.
- The bid envisaged that 80 per cent of athletes would be within 20 minutes of their events and 97 per cent would be within 30 minutes of their events.
- It was estimated that 80 per cent of spectators would arrive by rail and 100 per cent of spectators would arrive by public transport.
- The House of Commons Transport Committee published a report in March 2006 – *Going for Gold: Transport for London* – which stated that: 'Excellent transport will be a key factor in running successful Olympic and Paralympic Games'.
- The Olympic Games is the world's largest sporting event with over 200 competing nations, 16,000 athletes and team officials, and 26 sports.
- Almost 10 million ticketed spectators were expected to attend the Games.
- The Paralympic Games involves the participation of an estimated 150 countries, 4,500 athletes, and 3,000 officials and members of staff.

Winning the bid

On 6 July 2005, the International Olympic Committee (IOC) chose London as the setting for the Games of the 30th Olympiad and the 14th Paralympic Games. The city beat rival bids from Paris, Madrid, Moscow and New York, emerging as the winner after a tense fourth, and final, ballot. The success meant London would be the first city to host the Games three times.

The bid's success celebrations fell abruptly silent the next day, 7 July 2005, when terrorism struck the heart of the Capital. Three bombs exploded in quick succession on the London Underground, followed by a further bomb detonated on a bus in Tavistock Square. Fifty-six people died, including the four suicide bombers. More than 700 people suffered physical and psychological injury.

Despite the horror arising from the events of that day, Londoners showed a remarkable resilience, determined that their lives would not change because of terrorism. For London 2012 organisers, there was no greater reason to create a Games that would show the Capital at its best: unified yet diverse and open to the world.

Meeting the promise

Having achieved a successful bid for the Games, it was time to make the plans for London's transport a reality.

A central, persuasive argument for hosting the Games in London was making the city the backdrop for as many sporting events as possible. The proposal identified 12 main venues within the heart of London, plus a host of road events including cycling and running.

And while the Paralympic Games were a smaller event in scale, its geographic concentration at venues in the City and east London meant that, in crucial areas, transport would experience demand pressures equal to that of the Olympic Games. Moreover, the Paralympics coincided with schools returning for the autumn term. There would be little extra capacity gained from commuters taking holidays.

It was time for Transport for London and its partners to bring together an ambitious programme of transport investment; one that would not only help the Capital produce a sporting spectacular of world-class standard, but that would leave a legacy of transport improvements to benefit Londoners for years to come.

The cost: £6.5bn. The time available: seven years.

For the Games ... and beyond

While many of the plans to improve public transport in London already had agreement, confirmation that London would host the Olympic and Paralympic Games in 2012 meant increased and advanced funding to bring forward these redevelopment and investment ideas. London Underground benefited from improvements, including advanced signalling technology allowing for faster journeys and more frequent services. Those areas identified for upgrades were the Central, Jubilee and Victoria lines.

The budget also included provision to expand passenger capacity on the Docklands Light Railway (DLR) by 50 per cent, with longer trains and new stretches of line to Woolwich and Stratford International. Overground services would also undergo extensions and redevelopment.

Plans included a massive facelift for King's Cross St Pancras, a full accessibility programme of works for Green Park Underground station and a new bus terminus for London Bridge station. The jewel in the programme of works was a new transport hub based in Stratford, helping to seal the area's regeneration and unlock its full socio-economic potential.

On the roads there were plans for cleaner, more efficient buses, investment in more cycling lanes and a bike hire scheme, and new ways to tackle traffic congestion.

6 July 2005: Londoners rejoice in Trafalgar Square on hearing that their city has been chosen to host the 2012 Games

Opposite and right: While Green Park Underground station would undergo renovation, becoming a fully step-free station, the Jubilee line would become faster, better and more reliable. New signalling from Stanmore to Stratford would cut journey times by up to 22 per cent.

Below: The first train running on the new signalling system. London Underground converted the Jubilee line to automatic train operation. The underlying signalling and train control protection system is called TBTC, standing for Transmission-Based Train Control. More trains were added in March 2012 and this resulted in a 33 per cent increase in peak-hour capacity, space for an extra 12,500 passengers.

Bigger, wider, higher: 47 new trains for the Victoria line came into service in 2009. They have dedicated spaces for wheelchairs and baby buggies, CCTV in every carriage and push-button alarms direct to the driver. Special braking technology also means energy goes back to the rails to power other trains, helping reduce heat build-up in the tunnels.

The Victoria line also upgraded to 'distance-to-go' signalling, leading to faster journeys and as many as 33 trains an hour at peak times. Every platform, except Pimlico, now has platform humps, providing level access to the train and helping people with reduced mobility, heavy luggage or pushchairs.

Extending the Piccadilly line to Heathrow's new Terminal 5 (T5) included building 1.7 kilometres of tunnel. Funded by Heathrow Airport, the extended service was ready for testing eight months before T5's official opening on 27 March 2008. The new terminal increased Heathrow's capacity by 30 million passengers a year, and was to be the arrival point for many of the athletes' families and spectators.

Big and red, but green too …
London's hybrid buses reduce
emissions of local pollutants
and carbon dioxide by at least
30 per cent compared with
conventional diesel buses.

Above: Our transport partner Network Rail also carried out a series of improvement works. They upgraded the track of the North London line to allow longer, bigger capacity trains to run more often into Stratford station – with trains arriving every 13 seconds – and also added 'parking space' for freight trains to help keep tracks clear for passenger trains.

Opposite bottom: Transport for London and the London Borough of Newham worked together to upgrade Stratford bus station, with new bus shelters and better lighting.

Opposite top: A new ticket hall was opened at Stratford Regional station.

In 2010 one of Britain's busiest stations, King's Cross St Pancras, completed a ten-year £810m modernisation programme. The project created two new ticket halls, quadrupling the available space, and an improved interchange between National Rail, international rail services and London Underground services. All platforms gained step-free access from the street, with 300 metres of new passageways. The Grade I listed forecourt façade of St Pancras station also underwent restoration.

Top: The high-speed Javelin shuttle service operated between St Pancras and Stratford International, with a journey time of just seven minutes, providing a crucial link to the Olympic Park.

Left: The new London Overground route crosses over Shoreditch High Street. London Overground was launched in 2007 when the network transferred to Transport for London. Overlooked for investment for many years, the network was transformed into a quality, Metro-style rail service thanks to the extra impetus provided by the Games. Existing lines were upgraded, and a new route was opened between Dalston and Croydon, with four new stations at Dalston Junction, Shoreditch, Haggerston and Hoxton.

Part of the £500m upgrade of the DLR, the extension from Stratford International to Canning Town created four new stations and connections to five London 2012 Olympic and Paralympic venues. Capacity was increased by 50 per cent with the addition of a new carriage to each train.

Time to saddle up and ride your … bike. The Mayor launched Barclays Cycle Hire on 30 July 2010, with docking stations across an area covering 65 square kilometres of London. On 8 March 2012 it was extended from Shepherd's Bush to the edge of the Olympic Park. With their distinctive blue livery, 9,227 bikes were available from 576 docking stations in time for the Games, and a total of 14,513 docking points around London.

Tim Clark, president of Emirates Airlines, and London Mayor Boris Johnson at the opening of the Emirates Air Line cable car.

Sponsored by Emirates in a deal worth £36m over ten years, and delivered to a tight timescale ahead of the Games, the UK's first urban cable car gives travellers a spectacular, bird's-eye view over the Thames from North Greenwich to the Royal Docks.

Some 2,500 people an hour can travel in each direction, equivalent to 30 buses. Leaving twice a minute, 34 cabins complete the journey between Emirates Greenwich Peninsula and Emirates Royal Docks terminals in under ten minutes. The cabins are accessible to wheelchair users and cyclists, while children under five travel free.

"The Emirates Air Line is a stunning addition to London's transport network, providing a much needed new connection across the Thames."

Boris Johnson
Mayor of London

The final countdown

- There are 12 million journeys a day made on London's public transport network. On the busiest days of the Games an extra 3 million journeys were anticipated.
- £6.5bn was invested in upgrading and extending transport links to increase capacity and improve services across London and the UK.

These improvements included:

- An upgraded Jubilee line, delivering more frequent and reliable services.
- A 50 per cent increase in DLR capacity with the line extended to Woolwich and Stratford International.
- Extra capacity on the Central line.
- Refurbished and extended London Overground services on the East London and North London lines.
- Upgrades to national rail services on the Lea Valley and Great Eastern lines.
- Upgraded traffic signals and junctions on the Olympic Route Network (ORN), to enable traffic to run smoothly.
- King's Cross St Pancras and Stratford stations essentially rebuilt and expanded, with step-free access and extra capacity.
- Improved walking and cycling routes serving the Olympic Park.

The final countdown

In the two years before the Games, our preparations intensified. We hosted staff briefings and readiness exercises, reached out to thousands of businesses with travel advice, ran a high-profile integrated communications campaign, and guaranteed that our planning would make public transport memorable for all the right reasons.

While doing so, it was crucial to keep life in London 'business as usual'. Much of our preparation took place in the background, away from public view. Only in the last few weeks did our signs, routes and station livery transform the Capital into a clearly identifiable Olympic and Paralympic Games host city.

Throughout this time, our Travel Demand Management (TDM) team worked closely with the Olympic Delivery Authority (ODA) and specialist modellers within Transport for London. Together they pinpointed travel 'hotspots', the places and times when demand on public transport services, roads and interchange stations would be greatest.

Their evidence was crucial to our public awareness campaign, Get Ahead of the Games (GAOTG), and our preparatory talks with businesses and freight operators. It also helped us to finalise train service levels, develop station management plans, and identify only the most necessary bus route diversions, so minimising disruption.

The Royal Wedding in 2011, followed by the Diamond Jubilee celebrations earlier in 2012, provided us with perfect opportunities to test our plans. All these preparations combined to make London 2012 a 'public transport' Games, with record numbers of people travelling safely and efficiently across the network.

Strength through staff

More than just a 'job well done', we wanted to achieve our own gold standard for excellence in efficiency, communication and customer service. We held a special engagement programme, which included a tour of the Olympic Park. This was led by Mike Brown (Managing Director, London Underground and London Rail) and Leon Daniels (Managing Director, Surface Transport) called Fit for London, with the aim of helping our staff feel better informed about the exciting summer ahead and ready to manage as many as three million extra customer journeys a day during London 2012.

To give extra support to our front-line teams we also recruited, trained and kitted out more than 3,000 Transport for London volunteers. Each one offered to swap their regular job for stints as Travel Ambassadors and Incident Customer Service Assistants (ICSAs), supporting our permanent staff at stations and other key locations across London.

Keeping business moving

The 109-mile-long Olympic Route Network would be vital in ensuring all athletes, officials and representatives of the world's media got to their events on time. Thirty miles of the ORN included Games lanes to carry the Games family. A huge programme of temporary changes to the road network needed to be carried out with minimal disruption to residents and road users. The final installation took place over four nights, with additional road markings installed from 1 July along with adjustments to 1,300 sets of traffic lights.

We also carried out a massive information exercise with London's businesses. They needed detailed advice and guidance so they could assess the potential impact of London 2012, and adapt routine work patterns and delivery schedules to keep disruption to a minimum.

We prepared tailor-made advice for 550 of London's largest companies, and ran free information workshops and seminars for thousands of smaller businesses.

Keeping London's businesses stocked and customers served during the Games was a top priority. We set up a Road Freight Management programme, to help delivery services and the logistics industry plan how to time and route journeys in the most efficient way possible.

We also created a Freight Forum. This brought together businesses and the freight and logistics industries, the Traffic Commissioners, Transport for London and the boroughs, so they could jointly coordinate and prepare for business continuity whilst planning the necessary changes, including out-of-hours deliveries, caused by road closures for the Games.

Capital planning, nation aware

The GAOTG campaign made Londoners, regular commuters and people across the UK think about how the Games could affect their travel. Whether going to work or organising their route to the airport, we needed them to consider the potential impact of London 2012 on their journey and to think about alternative travel arrangements.

It was changing this habitual travel behaviour that formed the driving theme of the integrated GAOTG advertising and communication programme. The campaign comprised three key stages, moving people from awareness through to action.

We first focused on increasing general understanding about the impact the Olympics and Paralympics could have on travel, especially around main sporting venues. Next, the campaign prompted people to think how they could adapt their routines. We especially targeted commuters who would normally use or pass through one of the identified Games hotspots. The final stage of GAOTG encouraged people to actively 'make the change'.

On average, 35 per cent of Londoners changed their travel: by adjusting the time they travelled, using a different route or changing their destination. And 31 per cent did the same for the Paralympics.

Getting spectators travel-savvy

Preparing sports fans for their travel journeys, as many of them were unfamiliar with London's transport network, was another huge task.

To help, an online tool – the Spectator Journey Planner (SJP) – was created. The SJP's design allowed users to plan their route and method of transport, and to book tickets from any starting point in the UK to any Games venue. Launched in July 2011, by mid-September 2012 the SJP had been used by more than 2.6 million site visitors to plan their journey to see their Olympic and Paralympic heroes.

Ready for action

In the days before the opening ceremony, our teams set about positioning more than 215,000 distinctive magenta signs at or near stations to guide thousands of spectators to the 12 sporting venues across London.

We also opened the Transport Coordination Centre (TCC). Based at Southwark, this temporary headquarters for transport information was to prove an enormous success in managing the millions of journeys people would make during the Games. Set up by us in partnership with the ODA, it brought together, for the first time, 15 different transport agencies from across the UK, working together from a single hub.

The TCC swung into action on Friday 18 May 2012, when British Airways flight BA2012 touched down at the Royal Naval Air Station Culdrose in Cornwall with the Olympic flame. From that moment on, 24 hours a day, seven days a week until 14 September 2012, the TCC and operations centres played a central role in keeping London and the UK moving, while ensuring thousands of athletes, officials and spectators reached their events on time.

Left: Getting in shape for the Games. Our Fit for London staff briefing conferences made sure we were ready for Olympic action on the transport network.

Below: Olympic athletes also inspired staff by visiting stations. Here Amy Williams meets Nick Mersini, Customer Service Assistant at Baker Street station.

Leon Daniels (Managing Director, Surface Transport), left, and Mike Brown (Managing Director, London Underground and London Rail), below, brief Transport for London staff on getting ready for the Games. Over 19,000 Transport for London staff attended the Fit for London sessions.

"Work is already beginning on strengthening the flyover so that it is fully operational well ahead of the 2012 Games."

Boris Johnson
Mayor of London

Meeting the unexpected challenge. In late December 2011 a routine inspection discovered the 1960s-built Hammersmith flyover had developed a serious fault. Working day and night over several weeks, engineers replaced 200 metres of central reservation and increased the flyover's strength so it could withstand greater traffic loads. The repairs finished in May 2012.

Left: The crowds flocking to London for the Queen's Diamond Jubilee celebrations earlier in the year provided the perfect opportunity to assess transport plans for the Games.

Above: Table-top exercises. A model of London showing a travel integration map that displays key transport road and rail routes, Olympic sites and travel hotspots.

Top: A series of test events at the Olympic venues helped us prepare for the Games. We also included accessibility exercises to ensure disabled people could travel safely and easily around London.

The Get Ahead of the Games (GAOTG) integrated communications campaign kicked off in January 2012 and combined traditional print and outdoor advertising, radio ads, and online and social media communication. Stage one of the campaign provided one billion opportunities for people to learn how to prepare for travel during London 2012.

Plan ahead and get ready: Stage two of GAOTG encouraged people to think about ways of adapting their regular route to work.

Can you work from home on the busiest days?

Give the crowds a miss by working from home, or at a different location, a few days a week during the Games. Find out which days will be most affected and explore all your travel options at **GetAheadoftheGames.com** and follow us on Twitter **@GAOTG**

Follow us on @GAOTG

Don't chance it during the Games. Plan your travel now

The travel situation will change daily during the Games. Get help planning your journeys at **GetAheadoftheGames.com**

"We have two objectives — to deliver a great Games, and to keep London and the UK moving."

Sir Peter Hendy, CBE
Commissioner, Transport for London

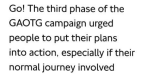

Go! The third phase of the GAOTG campaign urged people to put their plans into action, especially if their normal journey involved travelling through stations or transport hubs identified as potential hotspots for crowding and congestion during London 2012.

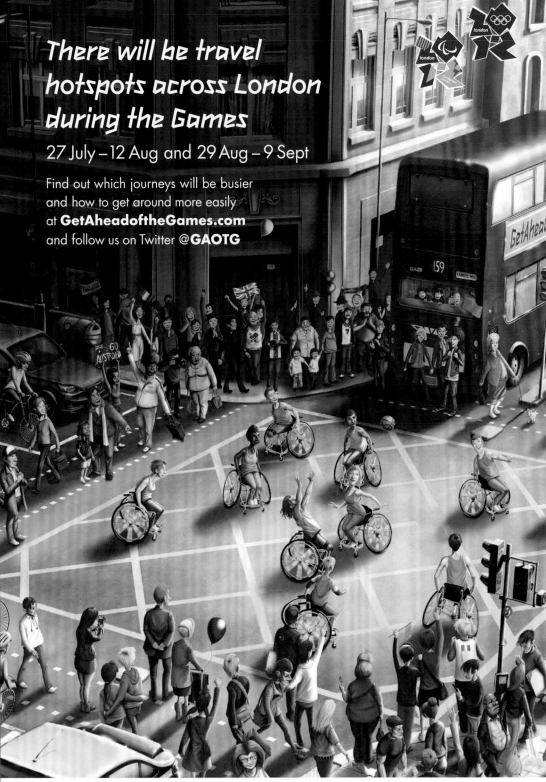

There will be travel hotspots across London during the Games

27 July – 12 Aug and 29 Aug – 9 Sept

Find out which journeys will be busier and how to get around more easily at **GetAheadoftheGames.com** and follow us on Twitter **@GAOTG**

Left: Peter Hendy (far right), with Justine Greening, the then Secretary of State for Transport (centre), and LOCOG chief Paul Deighton (left), fielding questions at the Media Centre in the Olympic Park.

Above: Transport for London holds briefings for the media and for business.

We began talking to businesses about the impact of the Games in spring 2010. From conferences and workshops, to direct mailings and advertisements in trade press and on billboards and radio, we got the message out. Nearly 25,000 businesses attended a workshop or presentation; 20,000 small or medium enterprises had a visit from a Travel Demand Management team member; we issued more than a million newsletters; and 250,000 companies received business advice packs.

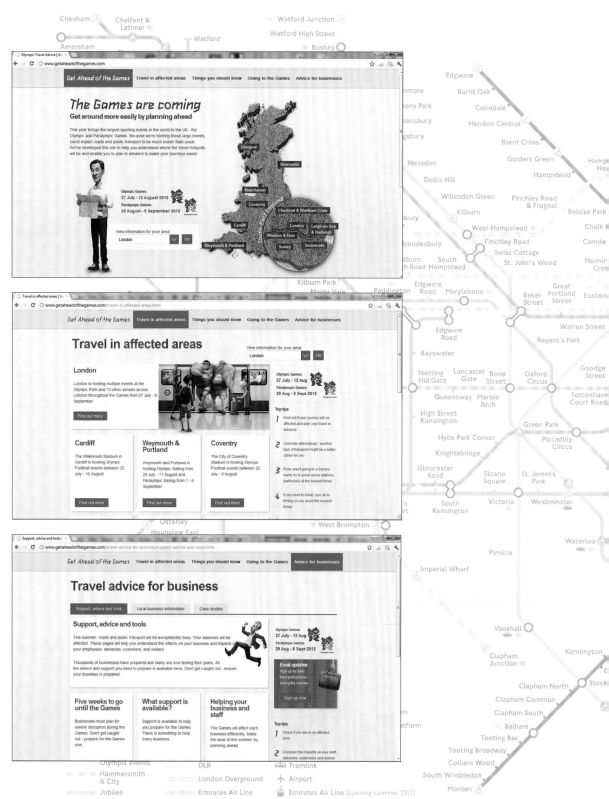

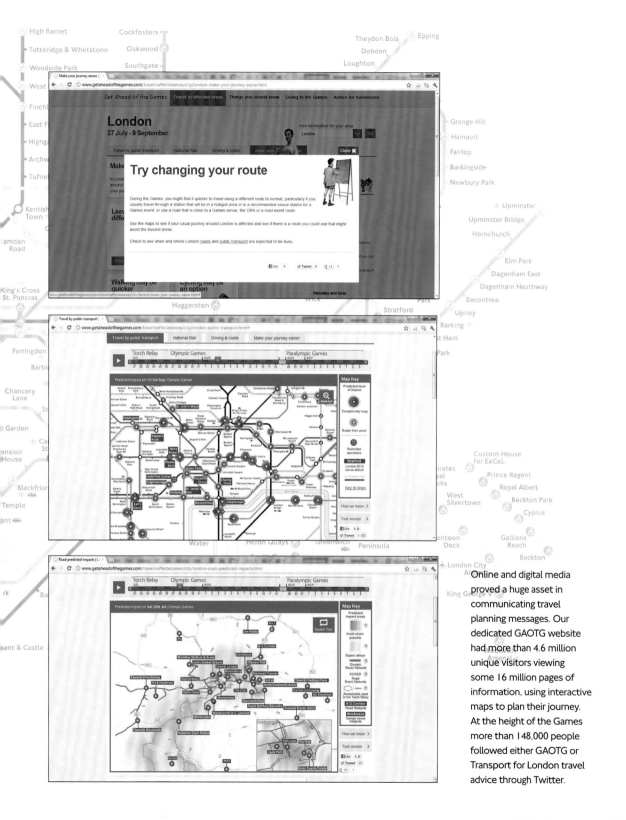

Online and digital media proved a huge asset in communicating travel planning messages. Our dedicated GAOTG website had more than 4.6 million unique visitors viewing some 16 million pages of information, using interactive maps to plan their journey. At the height of the Games more than 148,000 people followed either GAOTG or Transport for London travel advice through Twitter.

Jumping jacks! With just 25 days to the start of the Games, former Olympian Iwan Thomas teamed up with Transport for London to back our Get Ahead of the Games campaign.

For three days Iwan appeared at mainline rail stations, leading commuters in a series of warm-up exercises and inspiring them to cycle, run or walk for all or part of their journey during Games time.

Above: The cast of Shrek showing how Barclays Cycle Hire guarantees you'll make it for curtain-up.

Left: Send in the heavies … Weightlifters bringing to life one of the GAOTG adverts.

Opposite: The USA BMX team found Barclays Cycle Hire the ideal way to hit the tourist trail. And world-class freerunners 3RUN's spectacular and daring acrobatics made it just a hop, skip and a jump between London Bridge and Monument stations.

Freight deliveries make up 25 per cent of the weekday traffic in London, serving some 290,000 businesses and 7.8 million residents. To keep London moving we had to work with freight and logistics operators, helping them plan ways that would avoid hotspots and the Olympic Route Network, yet still allow them to deliver the goods. We developed a dedicated Games freight website and online journey planner, and created a tailor-made communication program.

Many freight distributors adapted their delivery patterns, often working out of hours and following a new voluntary code of conduct to minimise disturbance. Research shows 77 per cent of freight companies said they had prepared for the Games.

Above: Sarah Bell, Traffic Commissioner responsible for the Olympic and Paralympic Games, enabled freight and logistics operators to make the changes they needed to their operations through the Operators Licence system, in order to service their customers successfully throughout the Games.

The call for Travel Ambassadors received a huge response. We needed 3,000 volunteers from our office and support departments to join front-line teams and Incident Customer Service Assistants (ICSAs) to ensure help for travellers was always available. Our final volunteer numbers topped 3,200. All received special training, a Games uniform and technology to keep up-to-date with transport services.

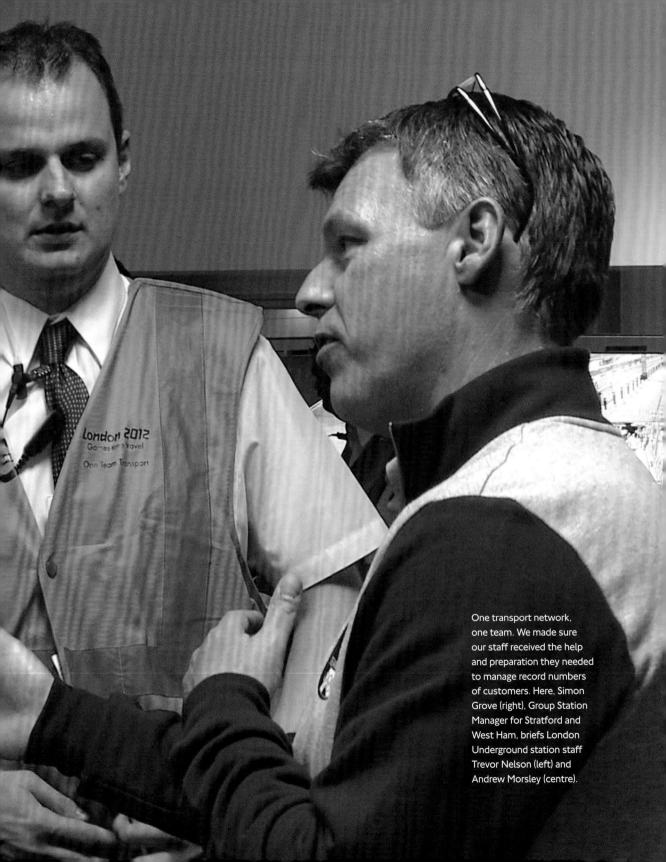

One transport network, one team. We made sure our staff received the help and preparation they needed to manage record numbers of customers. Here, Simon Grove (right), Group Station Manager for Stratford and West Ham, briefs London Underground station staff Trevor Nelson (left) and Andrew Morsley (centre).

Getting in the pink or, more precisely, magenta. Transport for London's Olympic signs became an unmissable feature about town, helping thousands of spectators find their way to the 12 sporting venues. On the transport network alone over 215,000 signs were installed and DLR stations were dressed with sporting images.

Road preparations included setting up 150 variable message signs (below left). These told drivers when the Olympic Route Network was in use or open for all traffic, and encouraged people to learn more from the dedicated website, getaheadofthegames.com.

Teams laid out Olympic lane road markings during the hours of darkness to minimise disruption and, prompted by poor weather, used special equipment to ensure the road marking dried for the morning peak traffic. They also installed road signs, advising drivers about lanes and time restrictions. The awareness campaign helped traffic levels fall in central and inner London by 16 per cent during the Games.

It's all about to begin …
The Olympic stadium during final preparations for the opening ceremony.

Meanwhile, the Transport Coordination Centre (TCC) at Southwark swung into action, ready to keep London moving. Set up by Transport for London and funded by the ODA, the TCC brought together, for the first time, the main transport operators in London and the UK. In the run-up to the Games, a number of test exercises were carried out involving a range of agencies including transport and the emergency services in the TCC.

The Games arrive

During London 2012…

- 62 million journeys were made on the Tube, 35 per cent more than normal.
- London Underground rapid-response units were escorted to incidents with blue-light support.
- London Overground saw an increase in usage of 47 per cent, that is almost 6 million journeys.
- Over 215,000 signs were installed on the transport network.
- Londoners planned their travel: between May and August over 62 million routes were planned on the Transport for London journey planner.
- There were 15 road events held across London during the Olympic and Paralympic Games.
- 94 per cent of Londoners surveyed in September 2012 thought Transport for London managed services 'very well' or 'quite well'.
- 83 per cent of spectators rated their experience of getting home after an event as 'extremely good'.

The Games arrive

Following seven years of planning and preparation, London 2012 had arrived.

Expectations were high, but many people remained uneasy about whether the Capital would cope. Could the city's public transport network absorb an extra one million visitors a day during Games time? Wouldn't parts of the road network become gridlocked by traffic? Would thousands of regular commuters change their journey to work as asked?

After the first one or two days of the Games these concerns quickly evaporated, with even the fiercest critics recognising the excellent performance of the transport network, especially the Tube, rail and bus services to the Olympic Park, and the lack of congestion on London roads.

This was not the result of people staying away from the Capital. Indeed, the busiest day in London Underground's history was Tuesday 7 August, when passengers made a record 4.5 million journeys. People kept travelling to work, but they heeded the messages in our integrated communications campaign, Get Ahead of the Games (GAOTG). Thousands simply chose a different route, travel time, or made walking or cycling part of their journey.

The effect was a broadening of travel patterns, rather than the spikes of demand normally experienced during the morning and evening peak hours. London's public transport network was carrying more people than ever before, but the spread of travel times reduced crowding and congestion.

Of course, during the busiest periods we ran more frequent services and extended service hours, with the

cooperation of our train and station staff. And our staff at stations and information centres across the Capital did a sterling job to help people find their way. Working alongside regular front-line staff was our army of volunteers, people that normally work behind the scenes at Transport for London. They swapped their desk jobs for an eye-catching magenta tabard and took to the stations and streets of the Capital with iPhone and iPads, advice, maps and suggestions for getting around town. With the Games Makers and Network Rail's Travel Champions they became one of the great successes of London 2012.

The bus network was ready to play a key role in getting Games staff to and from events, and contingency buses were strategically positioned across the Capital, for example at North Greenwich, to provide additional capacity it needed.

We also made great use of digital media to keep regular travellers and visitors up to speed with London travel. Our GAOTG website and Spectator Journey Planner helped people organise their travel plans well ahead of their journey. But we also expanded our real-time information, with daily emails to customers and updates issued through Twitter. We sent 60 million emails during the Games and, at its height, there were more than 62,000 people following GAOTG on Twitter, plus thousands more following other Transport for London Twitter services.

Taking care of business

Making sure London kept moving and working was a priority. During London 2012 we issued freight bulletins by email twice a day, at 4.30am and 2pm, providing the latest guidance on what was happening for the next 48 hours. This allowed businesses and organisations to cascade the information though their systems.

Because of this, and our public information to drivers, peak morning traffic in central London was lower than normal for the time of year. Many took our advice to take alternative routes rather than use Olympic and Paralympic networks, and avoid roads near sporting venues.

For drivers, the prospect of the Olympic Route Network (ORN) was a source of concern, and before the Games many believed it would worsen congestion. With the ORN being a contractual requirement of any host city, the key to making it work was good preparation.

We made amendments to road junctions, paint dedicated Games lanes road markings and carry out adjustments to 1,300 sets of traffic lights. Overnight on Tuesday 24 July, three days before the opening ceremony, we carried out the final ORN preparations, temporarily suspending pedestrian crossings and parking and loading bays, and implemented the ORN the following day.

While the ORN covered 109 miles, only 30 miles formed Games lanes. We set up 150 variable message signs (VMS), to keep drivers advised about when Games lane controls were in place or when roads were open to all traffic. During the Games, only 30–40 per cent of Games lanes were in use each day. The rest we managed flexibly, closing them to non-Games traffic only at times of peak demand from official Olympic vehicles. As a result, traffic around and on the ORN flowed smoothly.

Wherever people made their journeys, perhaps passing through renovated stations such as King's Cross St Pancras and Stratford, or using new train services or improved Tube lines, a team behind the scenes made sure everything ran efficiently.

Supplementing our existing operational control rooms, the Transport Coordination Centre (TCC), based at Southwark, brought together our Travel Demand Management staff with colleagues from partner transport operators and organisations. They kept a watch on the Capital's travel network, ensuring visitors, workers and businesses reached their destinations as easily as possible.

Transport for London Commissioner Peter Hendy gets behind the wheel of the open-top bus that carried the Olympic Torch along Oxford Street. And after the procession, relaxing on the top deck: Peter Hendy at far right, with senior management colleagues (left to right) Vernon Everitt, Leon Daniels, Howard Collins and Mike Brown.

"I've worked for London Underground for 49 years, so to be able to hold the Flame on its Tube journey is a huge honour for me and a moment I will treasure for the rest of my life."

John Light
Signalling Operator, Transport for London

Signalling Operator John Light, who joined London Underground in 1963, carried the Olympic Torch on the District Line, as part of the week-long Torch relay procession through every one of London's 33 boroughs.

Friday 27 July, the night of the spectacular opening ceremony. Some 80,000 people travelled to the Olympic Stadium through Stratford Regional, Stratford International and West Ham stations. Services ran until 3.30am to ensure everyone got home afterwards.

The 115-metre-high ArcelorMittal Orbit sculpture and observation tower, Britain's largest piece of public art, looks down at the stadium in the Olympic Park. Daring, funny and just a touch eccentric, Danny Boyle's opening ceremony, 'Isles of Wonder', gave everyone a night to remember.

"*The return to London of the VIPs after the opening ceremony coincided with the mass egress from Hyde Park. It was a huge concern – but we breezed it!*"

Leon Daniels
Managing Director, Surface Transport

The 109-mile Olympic Route Network (ORN) linked Games venues, accommodation and transport hubs around London. There were 30 miles of Games lanes to ensure Olympic vehicles delivered athletes, officials and the media to their events on time. The ORN was closed to other vehicles only when busy with Olympic family traffic. The London Streets and Transport Coordination Centre (LSTCC) monitored usage, which meant that for as much as 70 per cent of the time the Games lanes remained open to all road users.

Above and opposite: Many central London tourist attractions became Games venues. Hyde Park and its lake, the Serpentine, was the place to be to cheer on the triathletes.

Left: Transport for London was also responsible for preparing road events, such as the men's and women's marathons and cycling road races and time trials. From left to right, cycling time trial medallists Tony Martin, Bradley Wiggins and Chris Froome.

During the 16 days of the Olympics there were seven road events watched by an estimated 1.8 million spectators. Stations close to the venues saw a 50 per cent increase in passenger numbers, with the largest increase at Hyde Park Corner, Knightsbridge and Marble Arch. Tube services saw a 35 per cent increase in passenger numbers.

During the Games, on average there were an extra three million trips a day by public transport. Detailed planning and a huge pre-Olympics communications campaign ensured that both spectators and commuters reached their destinations comfortably, safely and on time. Train services ran one hour later over the Games and were extended to 3.30am for the opening and closing ceremonies.

It was a time for fun and patriotism, with every spectator making sure their national flag was on show.

Our maps and wayfinding signage helped spectators navigate their way to the sporting venues. We also set up pop-up information booths staffed by Travel Ambassadors.

Magenta was *the* colour about town.

As the Olympic Games were in full swing, the Capital was also home to world-class cultural events, and visitors and spectators found artists and performers in every part of the city. London glowed with fabulous light effects (as shown left on the Millennium Bridge), acrobats performed daredevil routines, and at Greenwich you could even walk around *Sacrilege*, a 'bouncy' Stonehenge created by artist Jeremy Deller.

Enhanced Olympic timetables resulted in a 9 per cent increase in Tube services. Reliability was improved, with a 38 per cent drop in disruptions. The net result was an increase in capacity of 11 per cent, space for an extra 488,000 journeys.

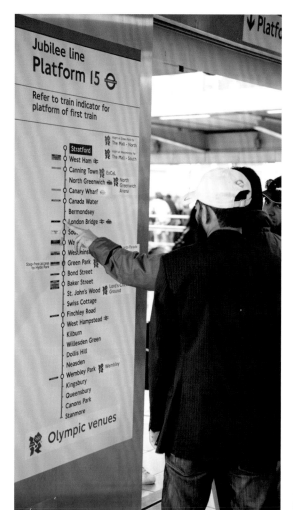

Stratford Regional and Stratford International stations were the main public transport gateways to the Olympic Park. The DLR saw almost 6.9 million journeys, a 100 per cent increase on normal levels.

The Emirates Air Line cable car, taxi, bike, bus, walking or train … both new and traditional ways of travelling around the Capital gave commuters and visitors plenty of choice in reaching their destinations.

By the time the Games arrived, £6.5bn of new transport and travel infrastructure was in place.

On Saturday 4 August, 45,000 ticketed spectators attended events, with another 231,000 people simply visiting the Olympic Park.

Behind the scenes. From the Olympic Flame's arrival in the UK through to the Paralympics closing ceremony, staff at control rooms across Transport for London helped the network to run smoothly. The Transport Coordination Centre (TCC) kept all the transport operators and the emergency services updated on travel performance.

Staff and volunteers worked together, ensuring people had the information they needed to reach their destination.

Opposite: Paralympic Gold medal winner and Transport for London board member Baroness Tanni Grey-Thompson with Travel Ambassadors.

Enthusiastic and happy to help. Our regular station staff, and ICSAs and Travel Ambassadors helped people find their way to sporting venues. Along with Games Maker volunteers and Network Rail's Travel Ambassadors, they became the talk of the town for their friendliness and one-to-one customer advice.

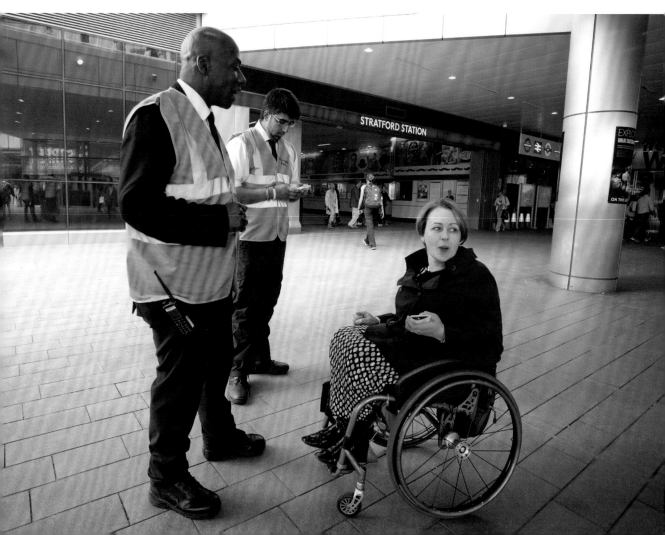

Many companies used the quiet of the off-peak hours to move freight and supplies around the city, reducing daytime congestion and avoiding Olympic hotspots.

Inspired by the triumphs of Team GB's medal-winning cyclists and athletes, many decided foot or pedal power was the best way to exercise and get about town. There was an increase of 24 per cent of people walking in the West End during the Games.

"Stratford bus station is already a very important transport hub in east London and as we move closer to the London 2012 Games it will have an ever bigger part to play in ensuring visitors have easy access to the Olympic Park."

Mike Weston
Operations Director, London Buses

Thousands of extra passengers used Stratford bus station during London 2012 because of its proximity to the Olympic Park. On average during the Games there were 6 million passenger bus journeys.

In partnership with the London Borough of Newham, Transport for London gave the bus station a full pre-Games refurbishment. We added new shelters, better lighting and improved footpaths, allowing passengers to move more easily around the station.

Moving on to the Paralympics

- By the time the Games began, around 25 per cent of Tube stations, 50 per cent of Overground stations and 100 per cent of Docklands Light Railway stations were step-free.
- Manual boarding ramps were introduced at a further 16 Tube stations.
- Almost 40,000 wheelchair users attended the Olympic and Paralympic Games – 18,000 during the Paralympics alone – with more than 2,000 wheelchair users travelling by public transport on the busiest days.
- 50,000 people lined London's streets to watch the Paralympic marathons.
- More than 80 per cent of British adults thought the Paralympics had a positive impact on the way the public views people with an impairment.
- The Paralympics saw a total of 39 million Tube journeys, up 18 per cent compared to 2011.
- Four million journeys were made on the DLR during the Paralympics.

Moving on to the Paralympics

Preparing London for the second biggest sporting event in the world presented a new set of challenges.

After such an exciting Olympic Games, including Team GB's outstanding success, people wanted the Paralympics to have equally impressive standards of organisation and efficiency. Transport was no exception, and with 2.1 million Paralympic Games tickets sold by 8 August 2012, we knew the demand on our services would, once again, put us to the test.

With most Paralympic sporting venues concentrated to the east of the Capital, visitor travel patterns would be noticeably different from the Olympic Games. We prepared for more intense pressure on public transport in this area of London, with spectators travelling mainly to sports arenas within the Olympic Park or close to the City.

Added to this localised, concentrated demand for services was the return of children to school for the autumn term. This took away the seasonal fall in regular passengers that was an advantage during the earlier Olympic Games.

In the run-up to London 2012 Transport for London had invested a significant sum to make London's transport network one of the most accessible in the world. Ahead of the 2012 Games, platform humps were installed at Earl's Court, King's Cross St Pancras and Green Park stations, as well as at almost all Victoria line stations. We had made our bus and taxi fleet fully accessible, the Docklands Light Railway was already entirely step-free, and we had created step-free access at all new Overground stations and 66 existing Tube stations.

To help disabled people unfamiliar with London's public transport, we created a series of short online 'how to' films. One film included a commentary by Paralympic legend, and Transport for London board member, Baroness Tanni Grey-Thompson. We supplemented this with dedicated information leaflets and posters at every station.

Help was also available from staff trained in mobility support and from our team of Travel Ambassadors.

During the period between the end of the Olympic Games and the Paralympic Games opening ceremony, we had just two weeks to transform London. Teams of staff moved around the Capital, replacing Olympic with Paralympic logos and branding, including wayfinding signage and station decoration, and creating the Paralympic Route Network.

This was a whole new event, with a distinct identity from the Olympics. And, as the biggest Paralympics ever, the expectations reached unprecedented heights.

Channel 4, the official broadcaster of the Paralympic Games, ran an advertising campaign called 'Thanks for the warm-up', depicting ParalympicsGB athletes waiting in a tunnel of the arena during the closing ceremony of the Olympics. It captured the mood of the moment. Everyone was hungry for more medals, new heroes and more great sporting moments. The London 2012 Paralympics would not disappoint.

"The London 2012 Games has benefited from the most accessible public transport system of any Olympic or Paralympic Games in history."

Mike Brown
Managing Director, London Underground and London Rail

On Wednesday 22 August, four groups of scouts struck flint against steel, kindling flames on the highest points of England, Northern Ireland, Scotland and Wales: Scafell Pike, Slieve Donard, Ben Nevis and Snowdon. These flames then progressed on separate journeys to London, Belfast, Edinburgh and Cardiff, before uniting at the home of the Paralympic movement, Stoke Mandeville.

Now a single flame, the Paralympic Torch then began a 24-hour relay to London, starting at 8pm on Tuesday 28 August. On the route, 116 teams of 5 torchbearers carried the flame past iconic London landmarks. Via the Docklands Light Railway, the Torch arrived at the Olympic Park and the cauldron was lit, heralding the start of 11 days of Paralympic competition.

"The Paralympic Torch relay is the perfect moment to get your flags back out and get behind the incredible athletes taking part as the excitement builds once again right across the Capital."

Boris Johnson
Mayor of London

A new set of advance warning signs helped people plan for the Paralympic road events. Signage played an important part in helping people find the most accessible entry and access routes. New accessibility signage was installed at 18 stations and 18,000 accessibility leaflets were distributed.

More than 2,000 people using wheelchairs travelled by public transport on the busiest days of the Games, and our knowledgeable staff and Travel Ambassadors were always happy to give advice.

In the run-up to the Paralympic Games we invested millions of pounds to make the transport network more accessible. Our improvements included making more step-free Underground stations, like Green Park, new lifts, better-designed trains, platform humps, wide aisle gates, tactile paving and audio-visual displays. The entire DLR was already step-free, and accessible improvements were made to River Services.

Funded by the ODA and managed by Ealing Community Transport, a fleet of accessible shuttle bus services transported spectators from the nearest accessible station to the Paralympic venues.

London's bus fleet is the most accessible in the world. All 8,500 buses are low-floor wheelchair accessible, and fitted with ramps that are checked daily to make sure they are working. The iBus system also provides audio and visual information for hearing- and sight-impaired customers.

The road events were a huge draw – on Sunday 9 September an estimated 50,000 spectators roared on the Paralympians taking part in the men's and women's marathon races.

Opposite and above (top and left): Spectators arriving for the Paralympic Games at Stratford Regional station, with signage in place to manage customer flows.

Above right: Spectators arriving at North Greenwich station.

A spectacular closing ceremony, with Coldplay, Jay-Z, Rihanna and a cast of 2,000 performers playing to a capacity crowd.

The countdown to Rio 2016 begins! The team from Stratford station starts the handover....

The Games Makers
cheer as they welcome
athletes in the London
2012 victory parade.

Monday 10 September was the chance to honour and salute the incredible success of Team GB and ParalympicsGB athletes, as they paraded through the streets of London aboard a fleet of 21 floats. The Red Arrows performed a tribute fly-past during the parade.

A lasting legacy for London

- Extra capacity on the Jubilee and Victoria lines, with upgraded signalling that allows more frequent trains.
- Extra capacity on the Central line.
- A central London Underground step-free accessibility hub at Green Park, plus step-free access at 66 stations and manual boarding ramps at 16 stations.
- A 50 per cent increase in DLR capacity, with lines extended to Woolwich and Stratford International.
- Refurbished and extended London Overground services on the East London and North London lines.
- Upgrades to national rail services on the Lea Valley and Great Eastern lines.
- Upgraded traffic signals and junctions.
- King's Cross St Pancras and Stratford Regional stations renovated and expanded, with step-free access and extra capacity.
- Improved walking and cycling routes serving the Olympic Park, now the Queen Elizabeth Olympic Park.
- Barclays Cycle Hire extended to Stratford, with 4,824 docking points in east London.

A lasting legacy for London

The 2012 Olympic and Paralympic Games were a great success for London and for its transport system. Over 10 million spectators attended ticketed events across the Capital, and almost two million more people lined the streets to watch world-class sporting action free of charge. All this resulted in record-breaking usage of the city's public transport system. Despite the pressure, the system performed excellently, winning praise from Londoners, spectators, athletes, the International Olympic Committee, the Olympic family and the media, setting new standards of convenience, reliability and customer service.

Yet the real test of the Games is what they will do for London over the coming years. Legacy has been fundamental to London 2012 ever since the city's bid was conceived ten years ago, and transport, in particular, was central to delivering not only a successful Games, but a valuable legacy for London.

New infrastructure

The choice of Stratford as the site of the Olympic Park was underpinned by improvements to the transport system. With the upgraded Jubilee line, the extended and improved DLR and London Overground networks, High Speed One, and a transformed bus station, Stratford is now one of the best-connected transport hubs in the country. East London is also benefiting from a network of new and enhanced cycling and walking routes and the extension of Barclays Cycle Hire as far as the Olympic Park.

Improvements in east London were part of the wider £6.5bn transport infrastructure investment made in time for the Games. On the Tube, the Jubilee line upgrade has delivered 33 per cent more capacity, while the Victoria and Central lines now both run 33 and 30 trains per hour respectively at peak times. The DLR has been extended to Woolwich and Stratford International, and benefits from new three-car trains, providing 50 per cent more capacity.

The London Overground network has been transformed, with brand-new trains, stations and track, creating an integrated Metro-style network and London's first orbital railway.

On the roads, investment in advanced traffic-signal technology called SCOOT and a programme of Active Traffic Management – probably the largest such scheme in the world – will also leave a legacy of improved traffic management and smoother traffic flow across the city.

Improved operations

Infrastructure investment is crucial, but the transport legacy of the Games will be greater than just new routes and equipment. The effectiveness of transport at Games time was built upon innovative and better ways of working, which TfL is now embedding into its everyday operations.

Reliability during the Games was excellent, thanks to a range of measures undertaken by TfL before and during the event. For example, the Tube's Emergency Response Unit (ERU) travelled to fix signal, track and train problems under 'blue light' conditions, driven by British Transport Police officers, increasing responsiveness to incidents, and extra spare parts were stored across the network for rapid deployment. TfL is pursuing these and other measures after the Games, looking to build on existing reliability improvements of around 40 per cent since 2007/08.

Journeys made on the Tube during the Olympic Games were up 35 per cent on normal levels, and London Overground and the DLR experienced increases of 47 per cent and 100 per cent respectively. These figures demonstrate that there is spare capacity on existing infrastructure, but network synergies, optimisation and behavioural changes need to be undertaken in order for it to be fully utilised. Work is being undertaken across TfL to ensure that lessons from the Games are identified and acted upon.

Volunteers

Following the success of the Travel Ambassador and Incident Customer Service Assistant volunteering programmes during the Games, Transport for London is also exploring the greater use of volunteer back-office staff in customer-facing roles, to support exceptional customer experience and create development opportunities. A volunteering strategy is being developed, and volunteers already supported busy locations over Christmas 2012, New Year 2013 and other major London events.

Transport coordination

The Games significantly changed how TfL worked internally and with external partners. This collaboration across the transport domain included the Transport Coordination Centre (TCC), Zonal Event Liaison Team (ZELT), and the Surface Strategic Command (SSC), introduced to oversee the expanded remit of the numerous operational areas in

Surface Transport. Following a review, the multi-agency collaborative approach across the transport domain will be progressed by a SSC-type function working across TfL. There will also be a permanent Event Liaison Team (ELT) facility in Southwark that will be maintained and managed by TfL and available to boroughs and events companies to support their operations.

Signage
Following the success of the integrated magenta Games signage scheme, a comprehensive review of signage on the Transport for London network is now underway. The review is considering the end-to-end customer experience of signage in key interchange locations, the quality of accessibility signage across the network, and using temporary or permanent Games-style signs to improve wayfinding for major events, both in TfL locations and in public areas.

Accessibility
Transport for London is also pursuing continued improvements to the accessibility of the transport system, building on a number of measures undertaken for the Games. The manual boarding ramps have been kept in use at 16 stations, and plans for further rollout have been developed, while signage showing wheelchair users which carriage to board has been retained at Jubilee line stations. Work is now underway to implement this at further stations, and a trial of permanent platform markings will follow.

Travel Demand Management
Transport for London cannot cement a transport legacy for London all by itself, of course. Guided by the successful Get Ahead of the Games campaign, businesses, freight and logistics operators and customers also played their vital part, re-timing, re-routing or reducing their travel,

or switching mode, to help keep the city moving during the Games. TfL is now planning to use Travel Demand Management (TDM) in the future. By making the most of new media technology and more flexible work and travel patterns, TDM can help alleviate transport pressure, and manage incidents, closures and events more effectively. This has already been seen in the public communication for the 12-day closure of the Central line Hainault loop, and Transport for London is now working with Network Rail and train operating companies to use TDM to manage the impact of major redevelopments including London Bridge station.

Cycling

The success of British cyclists in 2012 creates an opportunity to drive more active travel among Londoners. The new and improved cycling routes around the Queen Elizabeth Olympic Park will benefit the local community for years to come. Transport for London is expanding Barclays Cycle Hire, constructing new Barclays Cycle Superhighways, creating a substantially segregated route from the western suburbs through the heart of London to Canary Wharf and east to Barking, undertaking a major junction review, and giving continued support for cycle training. In the summer of 2013, London will also see a major new elite and participation event, Prudential RideLondon, which aims to be the largest event of its kind and to promote cycling to novices and enthusiasts alike.

Freight

Transport for London is also continuing its engagement with freight operators and businesses, including maintaining an industry-led Freight Forum, to build on innovative and flexible freight practices employed during the Games. Twice as many freight operators as usual undertook out-of-hours deliveries during the Games, and a quarter of those who introduced or increased out-of-hours deliveries intend to

continue in the future. Given that freight represents 25 per cent of road traffic in central London, increased use of quiet out-of-hours deliveries could have a marked impact on congestion, without disturbing residents.

The Games proved we can plan, build and operate a network able to support the most challenging logistical exercise a city can undertake. It also showcased London globally – demonstrating it is vital that investment in the city and its transport network continues, making London an attractive place to live, work and invest in. Most importantly, the Games have left us with the legacy of knowing how much we can achieve together and the need to celebrate our role in keeping London moving, not just during the Games, but every single day.

Journeys

35%
of Londoners changed
the way they travelled
during the Olympics

100%
increase in journeys
on the DLR, a total
of 6.9m journeys

6m
Number of
bus journeys on
2 August 2012

**Almost
6million**
journeys on London
Overground, up 47%

30%
of Londoners
needed to change
the way they
travelled during
the Games

15million
Total number of journeys made
on the busiest day of the Games,
3m more than a normal day

62million
The total number of journeys
on the Tube during the Games

Capacity

12,500
The number of extra passengers per hour on the Jubilee line due to capacity increase

47 new trains
on the Victoria line

1,300
The number of traffic signals to be upgraded

50%
Capacity increase on the DLR

33%
Jubilee line capacity increase in the peak

38%
Improvement in Tube reliability

£6.5bn
Total amount invested in upgrading and extending the transport network

9%
services increase due to extended operating hours on the Tube

488,000
Number of journeys as a result of increased capacity and reliability

13 seconds
The time duration between trains arriving at Stratford Regional

109 miles
Olympic Route Network length

65km²
The amount of London covered by Barclays Cycle Hire

14,513
Barclays Cycle Hire docking points

Barclays Cycle Hire bikes available **9,227**

Index

Picture credits

All photographs and artwork © Transport for London –
James Andrews, Ian Bell, Martin Breschinski, Rob Cadman/
Construction Photography, Paul Curtis, Michael Garnett, Justin
Grainge, Ross Holdstock, Jon Hunter, Luca Marino, Rich Maskey,
Thomas Riggs, Darren Ruane, Graham Stephens, Peter Stevens,
John Sturrock, Brandon Swartz – except for:

p.4: © GLA
p.12–13: © Adrian Dennis/AFP/Getty Images
p.20: © Michael Walter/Troika
p.36 Adam Cash
p.48: © Elsa/Getty Images
p.54–5: © Jeff Moore/Saatchi & Saatchi
p.59: Sir Peter Hendy, CBE
p.90: © GLA
p.91 top: © Julian Andrews/GLA
p.91 bottom: © GLA
p.126 top: © Dan Kitwood/Getty Images
p.127 top: © Jeff J. Mitchell/Getty Images

Get Ahead of the Games campaign
M&C Saatchi. Design and realisation: tokyoplastic with
Picasso Pictures Ltd.

Text © Transport for London

Published in 2013 by
Laurence King Publishing
361–373 City Road
London EC1V 1LR
United Kingdom
T +44 20 7841 6900
F +44 20 7841 6910
enquiries@laurenceking.com
www.laurenceking.com

A catalogue record for this book is available from the
British Library.

ISBN: 978 1 78067 274 8

Transport for London: Julie Dixon, Mark Evers,
  Paul Curtis and David Ellis
Commissioning editor: Philip Cooper, LKP
Senior editor: Melissa Danny, LKP
Text: Kay Pringle at Marmalade Keyboard
Design: The Urban Ant Ltd

Printed by Butler Tanner & Dennis, England

Front cover/title page poster: Denise Jacobs, TfL Design